I Like Dogs

Angela Aylmore

Heinemann Library
Chicago, Illinois

Customer Service 888–454–2279
Visit our website at www.heinemannlibrary.com

Photo research by Erica Newbery
Designed by Joanna Hinton-Malivoire
Printed in China by South China Printing Company Limited

11 10 09 08 07
10 9 8 7 6 5 4 3 2 1

Library of Congress Cataloging-in-Publication Data
Aylmore, Angela.
  I like dogs / Angela Aylmore.
     p. cm. -- (Things I like)
  Includes bibliographical references and index.
  ISBN-13: 978-1-4034-9269-2 (library binding-hardcover)
  ISBN-10: 1-4034-9269-7 (library binding-hardcover)
  ISBN-13: 978-1-4034-9278-4 (pbk.)
  ISBN-10: 1-4034-9278-6 (pbk.)
  1. Dogs--Juvenile literature. I. Title.
  SF426.5.A95 2007
  636.7--dc22
                        2006024841

Acknowledgments
The publishers would like to thank the following for permission to reproduce photographs: Alamy pp. **10** (Dynamic Graphics Group/Creatas), **11** (Colin Hawkins), **18** (Andrew Holt), **22** (dog in bath, Colin Hawkins); Animal Photography p. **7** (Sally Anne Thompson); Corbis pp. **12–13** (Larry Williams), **14–15** (Roy Morsch/zefa), **19** (Jim Craigmyle); Getty Images pp. **4–5** (all, Photodisc); Nature Picture Library pp. **6** (Ulrike Schanz), **8** (Wegner/ARCO), **9** (Wegner, P./Arcolmages), **20** (Ulrike Schanz), **21** (Eric Baccega), **22** (huskies, Eric Baccega; St Bernard, Ulrike Schanz).

Cover photograph of a dog reproduced with permission of Corbis (Aaron Horowitz).

Every effort has been made to contact copyright holders of any material reproduced in this book. Any omissions will be rectified in subsequent printings if notice is given to the publisher.

Contents

Some words are shown in bold, **like this.** You can find out what they mean by looking in the Glossary.

Dogs

I like dogs.

I will tell you my favorite things about dogs.

Different Dogs

I like the way dogs are so different. This dog is a Saint Bernard. It is big and hairy.

This dog is a Peruvian Inca Orchid. It has no hair.

This dog is a dachshund. It is long and short. Some people call it a sausage dog.

I like this dog the best.
It is a dalmatian. It has
spots all over it.

Taking Care of My Dog

I really like taking care of my dog. My dog likes to play.

My dog gets very muddy.
I give her a bath to keep
her clean.

I feed my dog every day.
I make sure my dog has
water to drink.

My dog needs a lot of **exercise.** I like to take her for a walk.

Jobs for Dogs

I like the way that dogs help people. This dog helps a farmer to look after his sheep.

This is a guide dog.

Guide dogs help people
who cannot see.

This dog is a husky.

Huskies work together to pull a sled.

Do You Like Dogs?

Now you know why I like dogs! Do you like dogs, too?

Glossary

exercise activity that helps to keep an animal or a human healthy and fit, such as going for a walk

guide dog a dog that helps people who cannot see

Find Out More

Ganeri, Anita. *From Puppy to Dog*. Chicago: Heinemann Library, 2006.

Gillis, Jennifer Blizin. *Dogs*. Chicago: Heinemann Library, 2004.

Macken, Joann Early. *Puppies*. Milwaukee: Gareth Stevens, 2003.

Index

24